BLUE MISTAKEN FOR SKY

PREVIOUS WORKS

Landscape with Female Figure: New and Selected Poems, 1982 – 2012
Autumn House Press, 2013
FINALIST FOR THE OREGON BOOK AWARD IN POETRY

Woman in the Painting
Autumn House Press, 2006

The Other Life
Story Line Press, 2001

House Without a Dreamer
Story Line Press, 1993
WINNER OF THE NICHOLAS ROERICH POETRY PRIZE

CHAPBOOKS

What the Other Eye Sees
Wayland Press, 1991

Happily Ever After
Panhandler Press, 1989
WINNER OF THE PANHANDLER CHAPBOOK PRIZE

Living on the Cusp
Moonsquilt Press, 1981

AS EDITOR

*When She Named Fire: An Anthology of Contemporary Poetry
by American Women*
Autumn House Press, 2009

BLUE
MISTAKEN
FOR SKY

ANDREA HOLLANDER

AUTUMN
HOUSE PRESS

Autumn House Press receives state arts funding support through a grant from the Pennsylvania Council on the Arts, a state agency funded by the Commonwealth of Pennsylvania, and the National Endowment for the Arts, a federal agency.

Cover art: Brooke Budy, *Anniversary*, 2000, oil on canvas, 11" x 14" / 20.8 x 30.6 cm. Used with permission of the artist.
Book & cover design: Joel W. Coggins

ISBN: 978-1-938769-33-7
Library of Congress Control Number: 2018932246

FOR ROBERT KIRSCHENBAUM

"AT ONCE WHATEVER HAPPENED STARTS RECEDING."
—PHILIP LARKIN

"AMOR FATI."
—EPICTETUS

CONTENTS

THREE

ONE

UMBRELLA

That first wet winter alone
a man approached me
at the bus stop, offered
his umbrella—just raised it
over my head—and we began
a long conversation.

Before the bus came,
I agreed to meet him
for coffee—all this a first
for me, so recently divorced
and new to this city.

That man could have been
my ex, I realize,
hindsight now like a pair
of 3-D glasses, rendering
up close and clear
the double life
my husband led.

If he had been the one
at the bus stop, some
other woman waiting
as the rain began,
he would have made
the same gesture,

though the umbrella
would have been mine,
bright blue with white stripes,
reliable even in the gustiest wind,
and wide enough for any
easy accommodation.

PREMONITION

Dusk, and the trees barely visible
on either side of the two-lane,
west through the Rockies
in our secondhand Rambler
that growled through the landscape
like some hulking animal.

Our first trip together,
my husband's attention more on me
than on the darkening road,
our newness a kingdom
of only two.

From the forest edge a deer flashed
toward my side of the car,
almost grazing my window,
then vanished into the woods.
I gasped—amazed we hadn't hit it.

My husband said he saw no deer,
that it must have been a creature
I imagined. But wasn't that
its jaw I saw? Its blazing eye?

Our Rambler growled on
and I laughed. Not exactly laughter
but that giddy foreign sound
that seems to come
from somewhere else.

Like the *falling* part of falling in love:
You leap onto the road unaware
the lumbering beast
speeding towards you
might kill you.

A STORY ABOUT THE HEART

In the beginning I trusted
its fearless turning
and I followed.

But the heart thins
with each disappointment,
twists in on itself.

Then it flies out like the owl
that slammed into the windshield
the evening I was at the wheel
bearing his silence again.

We stopped the car, lifted
the still owl from the asphalt,
one of its eyes stuck open.

Even then he refused to speak.
All night he kept his back
rigid beside me. I thought of the owl
stiffening on the roadside,
and I could not sleep.

My heart turned inward,
a tympani of fear, his—
even as he slept—
a snake in striking distance,

its teeth all eyeteeth, its venom
seething in the wound.

And in the morning
more white space between us—
Cassandra with her mouth closed.

So I dared to open my own throat
but could not speak.

When he finally spoke,
saving the worst for last,
my heart, a hole at its core,

like that owl
struck without warning,

fell and fell

and was lifted for a moment

then left on the pavement,
even its shadow scavenged.

DEAD END

We walked the road again that morning.
Bees dipped in and in, center after center,
dozens of them, a choir of hum—
and with such purpose they seemed
part of the coreopsis yellowing
the roadside. "Flowers don't know
they're beautiful," he told me
after the argument, "don't care
if we think so. It's in their nature
to be beautiful."

What's in your nature? I wondered
as he scowled away, became
a speck. A copperhead lay
in the ditch like a cast-off tire.
A single red leaf dwindled
onto the road as if to signal
something important. Dust.
Departure. A telephone rang
from a house near the top
of the hill. No one answered.
Not a single car came by.

The bees dipped in and in
and disappeared.
We don't plan these things.
Bitter coffee one morning.
White lie of the moon
in the white afternoon sky.
A man smaller than a bee.
An argument that by evening
seems to come to nothing.
And the nectar, come morning,
that rises again to be set free.

THE RULES

AFTER *ADRIFT*, A PHOTOGRAPH BY RUSSELL J. YOUNG

At first it is all one
borderless blue mist
we mistake for sky
or sea

But stare long enough
and the eyes adjust
or perhaps the sun
begs through
reticent but steady

the way after sex
my husband sits
at the edge
of a bed where
someone else's wife
lies in the dawn light
as it filters through
the slow filigree
at the window
where the night before
the moon acquiesced
and left them alone

Only this once
she says

But he wants
more
though the rules
say otherwise

say two
are not one
say sky is one thing
sea another

DOUBT

It's like the wool coat my husband wore
that seemed to usher the storm
into the house even after he removed it,
its fur-lined collar and cuffs made
to keep out the cold.
Icy air entered the house with him,
spreading its molecules of bitterness
into the room, its molecules
of indifference. Even wearing
my flannel nightgown beneath
my thick robe, knee socks
and slippers, I shivered.

GRAMMAR LESSON

The word *lie* is a verb
that's also a noun: He lies,
and his lie multiplies.

But *to lie* also means *to recline*:
She decides to lie down again
on her side of their unmade bed.

To lay means *to place*:
As he speaks, she lays
her coffee cup on the table.

But *lay* is also the past tense of *lie*:
She lay there the rest of the day,
barely moving.

Laid is the past tense of *lay*:
When he left, he laid his house key
on the counter.

About the colloquial way
we sometimes use *laid*,
need I say anything?

AREN'T YOU TIRED OF THINKING ABOUT HIM?

My mind like a spider
caught in its own web with only
the wanton wind to strike.

Like a thread
hanging from the hammock
that cares nothing for the wind.

Or the blanket tossed over the back
of the wicker rocker on the porch,
the wind trying to make itself visible.

My mind like the dog
that tramples the sparrow
the wind dropped onto the porch.

Like the broom that did its job
and leans now
against the peeling clapboards.

Inside the house the clock
winds itself, and there is no wind.
I am the woman who invited him in.

AS IF WRITTEN BY THE OTHER WOMAN

I didn't know he was married,
didn't know I wasn't the only one
who believed he had landed
in my life like an out-of-season
blue heron, singular and sunlit
at the edge of a lake, a figure
in a woodblock print,
drawing the eye as if he were
the source of everything.
And it seemed that way—
that all the light I had given up
when my own husband left
had been gathered and saved
by this new man who gazed at me
so long I believed he returned
that light and shone it upon
the world as if in a still life,
the tips of the hickory leaves lit
brilliantly yellow, the maples
stunned orange or red, evergreens
greener than memory. So
when he took me from my misery
to the bed I thought was his alone
I gave up every secret, gave not only
my open body, but let him unharness
every protection. It would be months
before you discovered my presence
and I, yours. Like some innocent fish
that rises to the surface to see
the sky no longer distorted
through the rippled water,
you are a woman like me
who did not yet know
that beyond the surface
a man could lift you
out of your element
and eat you alive.

THE LAWS OF PHYSICS

First from the porch, then the driveway
I shouted his name, its single syllable
a stone I believed I could heave
far enough to stop him
as he walked and walked
with that purposeful slowness
I'd come to recognize, his back
a shield against my voice.

At the end of the block he stopped
like that ocean wave in the footage
we'd seen together on TV,
its pinnacle pausing
just before it breaks,
before the wall it has become
swallows the shore, the houses,
and of course the people,
no matter how fast they run.

A stone is denser than water
and I hurled it at his back.
Didn't I understand
the simplest laws of physics?
Throw a stone at a wave—
at its apex when it looks
most fierce—and the stone
will pass right through.

GREEN COUCH

That last day, before I told him
he had ruined my life,
we sat together for hours
on the green couch,
my favorite place in the house
when he sat beside me.

Tentative at first, as if filling out
a job application or an election ballot,
we made a list, trying to stay calm,
one of us claiming the car,
the other the truck, one choosing
the oriental desk but giving up the china.

Before he got up to go, I looked one last time
into his face—really looked—remembering
he was the man I once thought I'd be safe with.
I felt my bare arms against the back
of the brushed green velvet.

Then he stood, and I said what I said
wanting not to shout or cry
but doing both.
He shut the door, and I listened
for his truck to back away,
the setting sun to stop quivering.

Silence and darkness entered
together, and I stayed a long time
on that couch, his place beside me
now mine, no matter how empty.

FOR LACK OF WHAT IS FOUND THERE

"IT IS DIFFICULT / TO GET THE NEWS FROM POEMS . . ."
—WILLIAM CARLOS WILLIAMS

My poems used to hold
wildflowers in them and lichen.
They held the limestone rock
where mosses flourished
and the Ozark woods
where we built our house.

They held a woodpile and a shed
that held a can of gasoline
for my husband's chainsaw.
They held the saw itself
and the shriek it made
when my husband cut firewood,
and that odor of fresh-cut oak
and juniper and pine.

Winter after winter my poems
held the warmth of wood
burning in our fireplace.
And when the wood turned to ash
they held the sound of the broom
as I swept the hearth clean.

My poems held the house, too,
and the marriage that thrived
for years inside it, even when
the marriage faltered, even
when it was felled.

STEPPING INTO THE BATHTUB

When the phone rang, you'd have thought
I'd step out again, I'd been expecting
the call so long. Instead, I stood in the tub,
remembered single words he'd used:
trapped and *met* and *somebody*,
which I heard as two words:
some and *body*, my own body
no more than what I glimpsed
in the bathroom mirror.

When the ringing stopped
and the answering machine broke in,
I heard my own voice, then his,
hesitant at first, then insistent,
apologizing again, then asking
when he could come by,
pick up some of his things.

When my mother died,
my father quickly packed
my mother's clothes and shoes,
even the bottles of perfume
she'd kept on the bathroom vanity,
as if he could not bear a single
reminder. I understood this now.

My husband's voice still droning
from the answering machine, steam
fogging the bathroom mirror, I lowered
my body into the tub, lay back,
let the water's heat comfort me
as long as it could.

FUNERAL IN VERMONT

JAMES FITZGERALD, WATERCOLOR

In the painting, a piercing wind
hurls snow against a little white church,
the light gray casket snow-covered,
the dark gray pallbearers and mourners
lined up behind them like tombstones,
their bodies bent against the sleetish wind,
all of them weighed down by snow
and sorrow, which is white and deep.

A book of the painter's work in my lap,
I sit alone now in my living room,
having arranged and rearranged my half
of the furniture, the wall behind me
empty of the painting it once held,
and through the picture window
everything summery and green.

If only closing this book would stop
what's happening from fully happening.
The artist has kept the mourners from ever
entering the sanctuary, the dead one
from being lowered into the ground.
Snow falls and falls, white upon white.
It neither accumulates nor disappears.
But I must go on until pain, anger,
sorrow, regret—whatever this is—
finishes with me.

AFTERWARDS I SEE EVERYTHING

as if through water,
everything that once mattered
now distorted,
the water sometimes ice
stiffening the view
I know might shatter,
or sometimes waves, wild
and unrelenting, forcing me
farther out, farther under.

The water never stills
and I don't know how I've been able
to hold my breath so long.
Even rays of light,
those fractured ribbons
that always draw me close
to the surface,
seem to bend
before they can reach me.

ARKANSAS TO OREGON

I kept the radio tuned
to the oldies stations,
one after another,
and sometimes, if I was lucky,
I'd hear "Blackbird"
or "I Want to Hold Your Hand,"
or another song I once loved.
I'd sing it loud
as if every word was mine.
This was the last day of my first
long drive on my own,
and I hoped not to stop
if I didn't have to, hoped
I could stay awake and alert
all the way to Portland.

For days I'd managed
to find music I could sing with,
even though I can't sing.
Or won't, if anybody else
might hear. But then,
at the western edge of Idaho,
the music fizzled into static.
I turned off the radio.
Wished I had CDs.
An iPod. Anything except
the nothing I had.

The sound of the highway
can lull you like nothing else.
Without music the pain won't let go
even though the landscape changes.
It keeps gaining on you.

Everywhere I looked everything
was brown. Gray-brown, to be precise.
Gray-brown hillside after hillside,
all of them vacant of trees.
The roadsides gray-brown, too,
and the highway itself. The sky
even grayer, browner, the way I felt
when I wasn't singing.

Soon the car would take me
through the mountains
and over the icy pass
and I'd be out of one state
into another. Geographically,
I mean. Trouble is
there would be no music
in the mountains.
I'd go it alone.
The way I'd been
going it and going it.
That's the way it's done:
You turn on your radio. Try
singing your pain gone.

ROOM TO ROOM

And then I began to muse, the way
all of us do who have been let down,
betrayed, left to wander room to room,
taking a stack of dishtowels from the kitchen,
packing the hand-me-down flowerpot
with its hairline crack.

Certain moments arrive abrupt as the siren
now blaring through the traffic signal
at Southwest 6th and Madison,
where the divorce finally delivered me.

To be clear: I don't regret anything
except the lost box of paintings our son made
of our old life. There was one
of our unmade bed, its blue percale sheets,
wrinkled in the painting,
our two haphazard pillows.

When he was young, all those mornings
he stood at the foot of that bed
and we invited him in. And later,

laughter, the three of us. Sunlight
warming the stone terrace.

If I lived there still
I would walk out barefoot.

A STORY I DID NOT TELL

The drillers came
with their giant machine
that dug and dug
and beat and beat,
the sound went on
for hours that day
but fifty, sixty, ninety feet
and the well was dry.

I did not say
my husband was out—
out of our house,
our woods, our town,
out of touch and on his own
the way he would be
on other days
as the men carried on
and the well was dry.

All I did was sit
at the window
or stand on the porch,
bring glasses of lemonade
out to the men,
tell my two-year-old son
why the pounding went on
day after day,
more and more feet
and the beat beat beat
we couldn't escape,
the well still dry.

My husband came back
and the years went on
and our son grew up

and the woods grew tall
and my husband left
again and again
my husband left
and I moved away,
but the pounding came
and the well, the well,
the well stayed dry.

TWO

FIRST SNOW

My friend said the first snow always felt
immaculate—she couldn't wait to play in it.

But she didn't grow up near a highway where
any accumulation turned gray before your eyes.

And she didn't have a father like mine, a man raised
by his mother's images of the worst catastrophes.

How can I forget those warnings he gave me
throughout my childhood never to eat it,

the way he forbade me to play in anyone else's yard,
told me that snow, no matter how inviting,

could be hiding something—
a broken beer bottle, a rake left on a lawn, a sinkhole.

Like those irresistible phrases my ex piled on—
how beautiful my eyes, my hair,

how much he loved, he said, to contemplate
my body. I should have suspected something

sharp and dangerous
below that gleaming landscape.

CONTRITION

I would sit in the second row
no one else in the church
while Colleen spoke too quietly
for me to hear
to the priest in the long robe
in the booth
I was not allowed to enter

What did I know
a Jewish girl
whose parents didn't believe
in religion
whose father had been bullied
on his way to school
by Gentiles

I didn't even know
what the word *Gentile* meant
not *Gentile* not *Jew*
the way I didn't know
all those Saturdays
in that town of my childhood
things I did every day
could be found on a list of sins

And I didn't know *sin* was also a verb
I would commit years later
in another town
on a hillside that first time
beneath the long branches
of an elm
with the man
I almost married
a boy really and I
only a girl

In Colleen's church I played
with the rosary she handed me
practiced saying words
she had taught me
Hail Mary Full of Grace
words that meant
nothing to me then
"Hail Mary" I whispered
alone in the pew
as if someone were listening
"Full of Grace" I said
turning the beads of her rosary
between my thumb
and forefinger

Contrition a word I also didn't know
Colleen used afterwards
quoting the priest
who told her
as if words could erase any sin
to say three *Hail Mary*s and two *Our Father*s
"who art in Heaven" I said aloud with her
for I too had lied
mostly to my mother
had said no
when the truth was yes

On that hillside
my body did the speaking
my body that refused to listen
to my mouth that lied
so easily I could take
both wafer and wine
and play at being
someone I was not

I had not yet learned
that whatever the body
takes into itself
whatever it gives
could also be a lie

as if anything said
or not said
done or not done
could ever truly be
Mother of God
erased or forgiven

ENVY

All our years of walking together
to elementary school and junior high,
I would race to her house next door
where she would take two stairs at a time
and join me where our lawns met
on Stanley Place. That day,
old snow lining the sidewalks,
I set out without her for the first time.

I crossed Lake Avenue and took the shortcut
through the park we both loved
with its little pond where sometimes
a few geese lingered, even in February,
and made my way to the high school
where out front I spotted her sitting
with her new boyfriend in his parked car.

I told myself again
I might have been the one
some boy had chosen,
told myself the rest of February
and all through March
when the pond ice cracked—
some mornings I stood at the pond edge
just to listen—

and kept telling myself on into April
when, one by one, tiny yellow crocuses
began to bloom there.

DRIVE-IN

All that summer I'm the one
in the front seat
beside a boy I'm bored with,

supposedly watching
Frankenstein's monster haunt the screen
or men draw guns at someone's corral.

But I can't help myself:
Through the rearview mirror
I track my best friend

and the one she's with this time,
their heads two paper boats
on a still lake

slowly drifting together
until on the other side a speedboat races by,
its sudden wake rocking them

toward one another, water
rushing over and over them.
And then from the screen

a woman screams
at the sight of the monster's face
or gunshots erupt from the dark saloon,

and when I look again into the mirror
I can't see anything, the lake
having pulled them under.

AGAINST SUMMER

Against only because it was the last summer,
one that began like every other, a summer

of evening light and fireflies. We all stayed out
as late as the parents would let us, summer

the season when they would merely glance out
and turn back to themselves, summer

their season, too. All those backyard campouts,
neighborhood barbeques—summers

that felt like forever until the light gave out
earlier and earlier, and summer

would thin into autumn and homework—out
of nowhere, it seemed. We longed for summer

to keep, as if that were promised, so we'd go out
onto our parents' porches and, hoping summer

could be summoned back, we'd still shout
across lawns lit by streetlights, as though summer

could be saved for us just by our calling out
to one another—*that* kind of summer.

But September taught me to doubt,
and what I had always loved of summer

died into October and took my mother "out
of her suffering," the rabbi said. No other summer

would ever come to an end without
my fear of what comes after, summer after summer.

BEFORE I KNEW THE DIAGNOSIS

Home from school and the house
so still that afternoon, only
the kitchen clock
and the constant drone
of the refrigerator, which I heard
as if for the first time
in the absence of everything else.

On the kitchen counter an orange
half-peeled and an open carton of milk,
toasted sesame seeds lying crushed
in a mortar, the unwashed pestle still
in the sink, and the pantry door
wide open.

Where was my mother, who never left
a room with anything undone?

I could have shouted up the stairs to her.
I could have checked my parents' bedroom,
listened at the door of the master bath.
Or slapped down my book bag
onto the table and left for the yard
or for my cousins' house next door.

But there was something present
in that room, something
in the sweet and tangy air.
Such stillness. Something
just begun.

I stood without moving
and breathed it in.

636 LYONS AVENUE, APARTMENT 1A

My grandparents chewed
with their mouths open.
I knew better than to mention it.
My mother, who'd grown up
in that apartment,
would not have approved
and would have given me
one of her knowing looks.
Stripped of hope this time
that she'd ever leave the hospital,
I'd come to eat with them,
these two who that evening
knew themselves
only as her parents
but seemed more like children
learning for the first time
appropriate behavior
as they sat at the Formica table,
paper napkins on their laps,
the meat on their plates cut
into tiny digestible pieces.

AGAINST SILENCE

After my confession I would stand
before my father at his office desk
on the first floor of our house.
And all I'd hear
was the scratch of his ballpoint
against his prescription pad.
"Yes," I'd say, "I did it"—I left
the mower out all night, forgot
to turn the sprinkler off, lied
about the party,
the pack of cigarettes,
the exact hour I got home.

His hours or sometimes days
of silence entered our house
like an unwelcome guest,
an intruder we agreed
to treat with kindness,
each of us saying *Sit here*
when we didn't want him
to sit anywhere.

After I apologized and promised
never to do it again, whatever it was,
after I made his coffee
in the morning, served it
with two Lorna Doones on the saucer
beside the china cup, sometimes
he would thank me.

But even then I didn't know
if it would take one more
silent dinner or two
before I'd hear forgiveness
in his voice, that other guest

who arrived unpredictably
while I wept myself to sleep,
that guest whose safe return
I prayed for, the one
my mother prayed for, too,
she told me later, that guest
she thought she'd married
in the first place.

EVENING MEAL

When my father was angry
he could not eat, and when he didn't
we didn't. I'd push a pork chop
from one side of my plate
to the other, the greasy
line of fat coagulating
on the white china.
Sometimes in the middle
of a conversation,
without our knowing
what had made him angry,
he broke into silence.
What had made him
made us. I'm speaking
of my brother and me.
My mother, on the other hand,
would continue to eat and go on
talking or what could have been
mistaken for talking:
Don't play with your food.
Don't line up the peas.
Use your napkin, not
the back of your hand.
My father used the back of his hand
the one time he almost hit me.
I had talked back, angry
at him, but also disgusted
with my mother for letting him
use silence as a weapon again,
his lips clamped shut
while she pleaded with him
to speak to her. My father's face
was white, its door slammed
against all three of us.

He pushed back from the table,
his chair thundering across the linoleum,
and I pushed my own chair back
answering his thunder
with thunder of my own.
Answer her! I shouted,
believing the words
of a twelve-year-old girl
could force open the locked door
of a grown man, as if
revealing this now,
all these years later—
in a poem, of all places
and both of them dead—
could change anything.

A THING OR TWO

My first time on my own in New York,
I stood as far back as possible
on the subway platform,

couldn't stop myself from staring
at the two teenaged girls dallying
too close to the edge.

I worried about the crying toddler
who clung to his father's legs,
about the old guy who kept gaping.

I hugged my shoulder bag
tight against my chest, looked
again and again at my watch.

Wind blew through the station
and the train approached.
When it emptied and man after man

crossed the platform to the stairs,
the man I was supposed to meet
was not one of them.

A bag of french fries lay crushed
on the platform, a wad of newspaper,
a wet comic book. And everywhere

the faint odor of urine. Then
another train and another, and still
the man I waited for did not appear.

This was before cell phones. Before
I knew a thing or two about the danger
of meeting a man I barely knew

at a place like that. I should have left.
But then he did arrive, this man who knew
more than a thing or two about a thing or two,

a married man, I'd learn, but would not learn
quite soon enough.

AGAINST THE LAW

NEW JERSEY, 3 YEARS BEFORE ROE V. WADE

My mother parked as instructed
at the north end of Grove Street and slid over
to let the man into the driver's seat.

She handed him the thick envelope of 20s,
which he slipped into the inside pocket
of his sports coat without even looking at it.

He talked about his son in dental school,
the price of his daughter's prom gown.
My mother spoke very little. I said nothing at all.

I watched trees slide by, traffic lights—
Did he do this for a living?—apartment buildings,
houses set farther and farther back from the street.

He stopped in front of a gray house
with a walkway that curved through deep green lawn
and told my mother to wait in the car.

Afterwards I lay on my side in the back seat,
nauseous and shuddering, my knees pulled up
beneath the lavender shirtwaist I never wore again,

my head on the bedroom pillow
my mother had thought to take with us.
No one spoke.

He drove us back to Grove Street
and, leaving us, shut our car door without
slamming it, but with the firm force people use

to close a freezer door, ensuring
all the expensive cold
cannot escape.

AND LATER I WILL FORGET ABOUT THE BREAD

I try to stop glancing at the clock, try
to focus instead on the task at hand, dusting
my palms with flour, lifting the round ball
of dough from the board, slapping it down again.

My son is driving home, his first solo trip,
his teenage eyes partially, I hope, fixed
on the highway's center line.

From my kitchen radio, Vivaldi's *The Four Seasons.*
I can never tell which one, the way I never remember
what Daylight Savings is supposed to save us.

I knead the dough to the music,
pick up the sluggish ball, slap it down,
push the heel of my hand into it,
fold it, pick it up, slap it down.

When my son was born he nearly died.
Now the clock declares him
five minutes late, then ten.

I place the dough into the ceramic bowl
he gave me for my birthday
and cover it with a damp cotton cloth.

The music moves from one season to the next,
the strings vibrant now and airy.
Twelve minutes late, says the clock.

The dough will surely rise. And spring
will come, then summer. But only
if the car pulls into the driveway,
his house key clicks in the lock.

TROUBLE IS

My father stands in the foyer
in his wool tweed overcoat,
his old fedora, its sweatband soiled
from years of refusal to replace it,
and his wine-colored oxfords
polished again this morning
as he polished them
yesterday morning
and the morning before.
Trouble is he won't be
going anywhere for hours
if he's going anywhere at all.
But no matter whether
my stepmother told him
to stay in bed longer
or tried to slip out
of her side before he woke,
she still finds him standing
in their bedroom closet
staring at the line of identical
white shirts as if one were better
than another, and she has to take
one shirt off the hanger
and hand it to him, walk him
to the armoire for a sweater,
tie post for a tie, dresser
for underwear, socks.
She's learned not to insist
there is no appointment
if there isn't. After all,
he can go to the foyer closet
by himself and find the one
wool coat, the one fedora,
the polish and cloth, shoe horn
and oxfords. And he can stand
all morning in the foyer
without any help from her.

BETRAYALS

At least my father did not betray anyone.
It was the plaque in his brain that betrayed him.

As for my ex—well, time passes, and I see
how some take what they need and even manage

to believe the lies they tell. That's as far as I'd go,
if I were writing about him.

Others don't know they're speaking falsehoods.
The year before his diagnosis, Dad began

to introduce himself as if he were still Lieutenant
Colonel Hollander, as if the next 40 years

had never happened. Perhaps plaque is so hungry
it eats away memory scores at a time.

It was summer and he stood at the front door
in his winter coat and hat watching something

through the little rectangular window.
Traffic? Children at the crosswalk?

Birds in the old cherry tree on the front lawn
we didn't know had been slowly dying?

My marriage was like that, despite its profusions
of blooms. None of us knew how soon that tree

would thud down during a late summer storm,
the tips of its branches scratching the front door,

my father's face framed in its window,
the few words he still knew—

hollow little grunting sounds, really—
escaping from his throat like birds.

NOMENCLATURE

In the forest where I used to walk,
birds peopled the air with conversation
I could not decipher
any more than the gibber
on a train through Kazakhstan.
Flicker or nuthatch, vulture or hawk,
I didn't know which song was which.

I, who can distinguish
iambic from trochaic, who can't
not distinguish them even
in ordinary speech, chose
not to learn their names.
I wanted my forest walks
unburdened by words.

Where else could my breath
be only breath and pass through me
with necessary inattention?

My father liked knowing
that a certain shriek is a finch's
mating call and not a sparrow's
alarm. Near the end, when he no longer
remembered anyone's name,
he made rasping sounds
at least his wife could understand.

I wasn't there. I was walking
in the woods, my breath steady,
my thoughts as empty
as the forest would allow.
If there were flickers
busying the branches,

they paid me no mind.
They no longer offered
whatever words
they once had for me,
a creature they'd grown so used to
I could have been
a woodpile. I could have been
a weed.

"MIND IS EAST HIDDEN BY TREES"

WHAT A FRIEND WROTE, MEANING TO TYPE NOT *MIND*
BUT *MINE*, REFERRING TO HER HOUSE IN A PHOTOGRAPH.

Each time we visited my father,
it seemed someone had removed
pieces of his mind's furniture,
but only one item at a time
so we didn't notice at first:
things rearranged but not
missing. Until one day,
no place to sit, we had to
stand with our bowls
in our hands. The next time
hold the food in our hands.
And later, no food—
our hands empty.

Then a series of rainstorms.
And afterwards a flood
rushed in and left behind
so much mud that even
without the furniture, we
couldn't get in—mud
that brought odd creatures
my father didn't recognize
any more than he recognized
us, his mind east, hidden
by so many trees
we couldn't see
the forest for them.

AGAINST RAIN

I turn right to escape,
but the rain follows,
torrent after torrent,
battering the windshield.

Wind blows with such force,
even when I'm stopped
the car trembles.

When the light turns green
a fury of crows rises
and flies somewhere else.
Where do they go
in weather like this?

I'd rather be home.
I'd rather be home
sitting in the armchair.

At the top of the hill
I can barely see.
I won't escape anything.
My father is dead.
My mother is dead.
I want to be home.
A frenzy of rain
rages across the asphalt.
The wipers screech and screech
against the windshield.

AT THE OUTPATIENT CLINIC

The young woman in the maroon hat
is tapping her left foot as she stares
into her empty lap. She's kept her coat on,
its collar of fake fur buttoned at her throat.
The woman's face is pale—*blanched* is the word
I was about to use, but my mother's name was Blanche
and I don't want to think of her, the way at the end
she grew so white and thin, her hair so black
I thought someone had rinsed it with ink. She lay so flat
beneath those hospital sheets, I thought at first
the bed empty, that they had taken her away.

Now a man I didn't see before gawks at me,
his eyes earnest, green, and stern like my father's.
"Angela," he says. "No," I say, but he keeps staring.
I'm saved when his name is called,
and he turns his head the way my mother did
that last time when I stood at the foot of her bed,
her name on a blue card inserted
into the slot beside the door.
She stirred when she heard my voice,
then turned away.

My mother's head of ink-black hair
on that bleached white pillow,
her name typed out in block letters
on one of those little blue cards.
What do they do with them
afterwards?

THREE

WHY I KEPT WALKING

The afternoon after the movers left,
I stood at the corner about to cross
Southwest 6th Avenue, cars purring
at the light, when a driver honked
and my heart lurched almost as it had
at the altar, my hands cradled in his,
the two of us who soon would kiss
in front of our family and friends
all those years ago and afterwards
would walk again up the same aisle
we had walked down, and for years
would walk down other aisles—
supermarkets and hardware stores—
and up the stairs to the room where a judge
signed the divorce papers, and I would leave
the house we built together, I would sell
the crystal glassware and the green couch,
even the desk I'd saved so long to buy,
and I would move to this city I had visited
early in the marriage and know it
the way Eliot knew you could return
to a place you thought you knew
and know it now as if for the first time,
as today, street after street, I passed
people in cars, couples at outdoor cafés
where I could have stopped and sat
but I kept walking—across the bridge
over the Willamette, from one neighborhood
to the next, the odor of onions grilling
and garlic, past tomato plants staked
in garden after garden, jasmine
and gardenias, roses and more roses—
I kept walking until the cars lessened
and lessened, I no longer noticed

how few there were, until there were no cars
and I walked without destination the way
when I had a car, before I moved here,
I would drive not to get somewhere
but to leave, to speed to a place
where I could be someone else,
and then I could park and walk again
and a stranger might look at me
and I might see pleasure in his face
as he stopped his raking or watering
or weeding, and I would nod
and he would nod and I could walk on,
and all I'd hear would be the laughter
of children in someone's backyard,
the occasional screen door slamming
and stuttering to a close, and I would remember
moments of my childhood when I feared
what would happen if I grew up to become
the divorced woman I sometimes glimpsed
from our living room window, how she walked
up and down our street day after day
as if she belonged.

LIVING ALONE AT SIXTY-FOUR

Friends said I'd hate it, since I lived so long
with somebody else. But on this first morning
in my fourth-floor apartment, I linger
at my kitchen window watching
the fog give way to a cascade of cars
entering the city over the Fremont Bridge.
A plate of fresh apricots glows
on my new table, its birch veneer
vacant of memory. Limes in a bowl
on the kitchen counter. Wine glasses
lined up in the glass front cabinet.
I love the way the dust motes shimmer.

AT THE GYM

A few of us lift weights.
Others run or keep pace
on treadmills, pedal
stationary bikes, stare
at television screens.
Bodies rise and fall
on moving stairs.
Alone, I lower myself
into the exercise pool,
swim in place against
furiously moving water.

A YEAR AFTER THE DIVORCE, I TAKE A LONG DRIVE

Just off the highway I find the bluebells
I'd read about, seen only on postcards
or calendars. Never have my eyes been so fed.
I step out into the almost silent meadow,
the commotion of passing traffic
diminishing as I walk.
A copse of firs stands guard.
A shallow streambed listens.
Birds are silent, invisible.
If there are rabbits or squirrels
they keep their distance.
I lie down in the blue
waterless river of flowers
like the child in the storybook
who hid among wheat stalks
wanting not to be found.
I lie there a long time.
Darkness sifts over me.
Stars poke through
and I am alone
in a way I've never before
been alone. And I understand
that although I've come a long way
from where I began
I have only begun.

PHOTOGRAPH OF A MAN IN A DOORWAY

One foot in, one out—
and out of view.
And behind him
a woman, though
the photographer caught
only one of her feet,
part of her leg.

Everything outside
where they hesitate
is bright, as if
cleansed by rain.
Inside, only darkness.
Perhaps they're coming in
after standing on the stoop
where a rainbow appeared.
Or maybe she stormed out
after an argument
and he waited a moment,
then walked outside,
sweet-talked her back.

When the man fully enters,
he won't see anything
until his eyes adjust.
I've been where he stands,
fulcrum or precipice,
one foot out, one inside
a place I thought solid,
a room I could enter
without turning on a light,
believing when I did,
the table would be
as I left it, candles
waiting to be lit,

wine glasses to be filled,
my lover behind me
reaching for my hand,
trusting my lead.

AGAINST DETRITUS

Yesterday I walked to the river
where the sun shone
for the fourth day in a row.

Clustered against the shore,
a few candy wrappers, bright blue
and yellow, a red plastic pacifier,
and something gray and stringy
I couldn't identify.

Some mornings I sit on a bench
beside the water. I try to be still,
release myself from what I know.

Other days I stay in my flat
and sit at the dining table
beside the window that opens
onto the alley four stories below
where everyone in my building
dumps their recycling and trash,
their glass bottles that make little
crashing sounds, glass against glass.

Some mornings the alley is quiet.
Some days the river is clean.

No matter where I sit
I've got the same job
of trying to clear my mind.
I don't want to think anymore
about what happened or why.

To empty myself, I write.
My fountain pen takes a small,
cylindrical cartridge of ink.

Like blood, it is dark
and hidden.
I must pierce it
to make the ink flow.

MELANCHOLY

A SERIES OF PAINTINGS BY EDVARD MUNCH OF HIS
FRIEND AT THE END OF A LOVE AFFAIR

The day after the exhibition
I glimpsed my ex from a distance.
He looked inexplicably ordinary
and so much like the man
staring out from each canvas.
Seated on a boulder, his chin
leaning into his palm, elbow
on his knee, the sea and sky
intensely blue in one painting,
almost purple in the next,
he broods, as if remembering
something he regrets
or tasting something sour.
In every painting his face
is stark, white, his eyes sullen,
no matter that the moon,
as it tries to get his attention
the way I did, brightens the water.

BED

I don't mind lying down at night
by myself, don't mind the absence
on the other side or the fact
of being alone. I don't even mind
that the man who used to
occupy that space chose to lie
in other women's beds. I like
that now I can stretch
all the way out, my body
in perfect proportions,
as if I were as balanced
as a planet in the cosmos.

Sometimes when I lie down
I think of the 35 years
of beds we shared, that first
foam mattress on the floor
of the attic room, the rent so cheap
we didn't complain
about the mice tittering all night
in the ceiling and walls. The perfect
Posturepedic we saved up for
and kept for years, the antique iron frame
I painted outdoors, only to discover later
the tiny damselfly imbedded
in the bar I grabbed during sex,
a death held tight in my grasp.

Now all the pillows are mine
and the cool place where the top sheet
touches the bottom on the side
that used to be his.
When I want that coolness,
I take it. No other body in the way,

no one else to be careful not
to disturb when I wake at 4 a.m.
And if I can't get back to sleep, I can
turn on the bedside lamp and read,
listen to late-night jazz on the radio,
then sleep as long as I damn well please.

Yet some mornings, rising alone
from the bed I bought when he left,
in the flat I found when I sold the house,
in a room he'll never see—
before I open my eyes, despite myself,
I reach for him.

IT TAKES TIME, THEY TELL ME

A cardinal flames from the bough
becomes the sun that so many days
ached its way down pulling me with it
pulling the shade my mother down
in her open coffin the dream
that kept keeping me awake
and the pit I thought would always be
like a stone I didn't notice at first
something cracking it apart tiny
green stem thickening yes into
trunk into tree I see first
one branch then another then
branch branch I see so many
leaves greening into green
into gray nest into flame that red dot
disappearing yes but how it ignites
I promise yes I will take whatever time
however long it takes
it takes

ANOTHER CALL

I was complaining to myself
when he phoned, this colleague
who called when he tired
of his wife's complaints about him:
his obsession with the telescope,
with football on television,
and the way her words *always,*
she told him, passed through the room
and out the door of their house
without ever entering his head.

His complaints about her
were echoes of hers about him.

About my own complaints
I didn't tell him: the ordinary
troubles of a woman living alone
after 35 years, the work
of getting used to having no one
to blame for anything—dishes
in the sink, the unmade bed,
the torn window shade,
the empty place on the couch
beside me.

When the phone rang
and it was him again,
I wondered if I was the only one
he called. And whom, I mused,
had my then-husband phoned
with complaints about me:
dishes in the sink, unmade bed?
Perhaps he chose the woman
he's with now because she listened
without complaint, as I do
to this man's everything.

GARDEN WEDDING

After their ceremony—
the obligatory poem,
obligatory solo, obligatory
kiss—after the champagne
and the first slice of cake,
I took myself away
from the crowd.

In the shade of a dogwood
no longer in bloom,
I spotted a chair, weathered
but sturdy, a rocker
that no longer rocked,
and I sat. Removed. Hidden,
but not hiding.

I could hear laughter and music.
I could hear the voices of children.

There's something to be said
for sitting apart on a late afternoon
after a wedding, something
about being what you can't be
when you're part of the party.
The flowers still bright and alive,
the radiant bride dancing now
with her father, I felt at the edge
of an essence I could not define,
the sun not yet blurring
through the hedges.

TWO

On the table, two eggs,
one a wooden imitation
of the other.

Outside the wind strips
the maple of its leaves.

In the book I'm reading
a man pulls into his garage,
sits in his car, studies
the backs of his hands.

The egg made of mahogany
and turned by hand
with a chisel and a foot lathe
is more lovely.

I knew this
when I bought it.

Outside leaves scuttle
along the walkway
and then are still.

On the next page the man
stands in the kitchen doorway.
We see him gazing
at his wife, her graying strands.

In a matter of days, the wind
will finish, leaving the tree bare,
the sky larger and cold.

When the man leaves the house
we will go with him, page
after page. About the wife
I will worry.

The other egg, gathered
from straw and still warm,
will not last.

AGAINST READING

Not reading, exactly
but reading too much
into what others say,
what they do.
Let's say your mother
shuts fast the book
when you enter the room.
Your wife slams down
the receiver. Sure,
if the dog scratches
at the front door, whines
and won't stop whining
you can probably
guess what he needs.
But maybe the book
your mother held
held no mystery
for you to solve,
no scene too racy.
And your wife?
Couldn't it be
that she didn't
hear you come in,
that it *was* a wrong
number again,
that trite excuse
this time true,
someone trying
to sell her something
you didn't need?
And that look
she gave you
the last time
it happened, her quick
retreat, her flushed

face, her voice,
her sudden need
to let the whining dog
out. To go out with him.
Why make assumptions?
Not everything is done
with you in mind.

GLIDE

In the checkout line at the supermarket
I spot a man I recognize from years ago
when I was in my twenties. Back then
he was the boyfriend of a girl I knew.
They used to skate together at the local mall,
she in one of those red velvet dresses
you'd see in the Ice Capades, her leggings
white and studded with sequins, a tiara
in her tied-back black hair. He wore
ordinary street clothes: blue jeans
and some unremarkable sweater,
which let her stand out even more,
as though she were a woman
a man like him could only
dream into being.

Today he's stooped and gray.
His raincoat so large, it drapes
over his shoulders making him look
like an afterthought beneath it.
In his shopping cart only milk, eggs.
On the ice he was the one I'd watch,
so unlike other boys, other men.
How unobtrusively he'd glide,
maneuver his partner as though his job
was to appear to disappear beside her.
I wish I could remember his name.

MUSIC

Was it raining? Was it raining
when he pulled the car to the curb
to let me out and leaned toward me
and kissed me not the way
I expected but as if we were lovers,
and I shook afterwards, shook
as I sat in the passenger seat
fiddling with the seat belt?
Was I still buckled in?
Wasn't it raining?
And the car—didn't it hum?
Didn't the windshield wipers
sweep across the glass
like a bow across strings?
Or was that the traffic? Or him?
Was it he who hummed
before I shut the car door?
Or was it I alone?
Did I do that? Should I be
embarrassed? Ashamed?
Or did we hum together?
And after he drove away,
was I that woman
who stood on the curb
of that crowded wet street
wondering if it was
music she heard?
That silly woman
who never opened her umbrella
as the rain came down,
pooling on the sidewalk,
rushing over the curb.

THE BEFORE AND THE AFTER

At the airport terminal the coarse sound
of wheeled suitcases, a toddler giggling,
running a few feet beyond his father.

A brown-haired woman at the kiosk
that sells last-minute magazines and candy.
I try not to gawk, but she looks like my mother.

I pull my own wheeled carry-on to Security,
lift it onto the conveyer belt, walk into the booth,
and hold my hands above my head.

I am always going and going.
The way my mother did.

After she packed both our suitcases,
I'd sit on the stool in the master bathroom,
while my mother brushed my hair.

I'd stare into the mirror at our two faces
so much alike they could have been
a portrait: *The Before and the After.*

She's been dead almost 50 years,
and I keep going and going.

From 35,000 feet I look down
at the clouds, the blue sky above so vital
before it blackens.

Then there it is again: just a hint
of her face in the airplane window
gazing back at me.

BLOSSOM

I was not alone one bitter winter night
waiting for the bus back to the city
from the outskirts. A tall middle-aged man
with a straggly beard, uncombed hair,
and stained trousers with frayed cuffs, paced
the empty street in front of me, smoking.
I doubt he gave me a single thought:
solitary older woman in a woolen hat
and long black winter coat and scarf.
The wind wheezed, and I wound
the scarf tighter around my neck.
The man kept pacing, smoking,
his ungloved hands red and chapped.
When the bus finally came he didn't toss
his cigarette into the street nor crush it
on the sidewalk, but instead tapped it
against the glass wall of the kiosk,
gently, until it was out. Then,
with the kind of care I once gave
the delicate blossom of a trillium
for which I'd scouted the forest
for hours, he tucked the small stub
into a pocket of his denim jacket,
and stepped up into the bus before me.

DUST

Every day, everywhere—
on the floor tangled
with strands of my hair,
in the corners, along baseboards,
on windowsills, bookshelves,
tops of the books themselves.
On stacks of papers that weeks ago
I should have filed. Even on the cloth
covering my father's Olivetti,
its last black ribbon marked
by his key strokes.

For Christmas my grown son
gave me a vacuum cleaner.
No more dusting corners
or dry mopping floors, he told me.
No more sweeping away
pine needles already dropping
from the tree.

It's late March and still
I haven't opened the box.
I would miss the broom,
the dustpan, dustcloth, dust mop.
I would miss the silence
that settles on me as I clean.

PLEASURE

Because yesterday I lay fully dressed
alone on my bed listening
to the sweet-tempered yatter
of rain I'd longed for all summer,
a sound that continued for hours
against the bedroom window,

and because the dissonance of traffic
on the street below was faint beneath it,
the rain light and steady and close,

and because yesterday it finally felt normal
to sleep alone, wake and eat alone,
walk out on my own, deciding
when and where to go
without telling anyone,

this morning, because I remembered
the pleasure of yesterday's rain,
yesterday's solitude,
I showered and dressed, I finished
my second cup, put the *Times*
in the recycling bin under the sink,
and took my time tidying the kitchen,

and then, because I could,
and because I no longer think of pleasure
as something that must be shared,
as I believed all those years
of my marriage,

I walked back down the hall
past new paintings by my son
and stood awhile in my bedroom
admiring the brocade coverlet

I bought my first winter alone,
its intricate stitching, its pearl gray sheen,
and slipping off my shoes
I lay down again and listened,
even though there was no rain.

NOTES ON THE POEMS

"A Story about the Heart" is an interpretive translation in poetry of a metal sentence sculpture by Steve Tilden.

"The Rules" is featured in and was initially written for *In the Mist: Giving Voice to Silence* by Russell J. Young (NotaBeast, 2015).

"For Lack of What Is Found There" is a phrase from William Carlos Williams's ardent assertion, put forth in his poem "Asphodel, that Greeny Flower": "It is difficult / to get the news from poems / yet men die miserably every day / for lack / of what is found there."

"*Funeral in Vermont*" is for my friend Cal Hennig, who wrote the book about James Fitzgerald and gave it to me as a gift.

"Afterwards I see everything" is for Chrys Tobey. An earlier version was written in response to a photograph taken in Iraq by Joel Preston Smith, who has served on humanitarian-aid missions in troubled regions of the world.

"*Contrition*" is for Colleen Albano Schweitzer, Kathy McMenamin Heery, and Patti DiComo Roediger.

"Envy" is for Brenda Hollander Gaffen with love and gratitude for gifts that persist.

"Against Summer" is for my brother, Gordon Wayne Hollander, and for Ron Hollander and Brenda Hollander Gaffen, our cousins who lived next door and without whom childhood would not have felt so rich.

"Photograph of a Man in a Doorway" and "Garden Wedding" are ekphrastic responses to photographs by Tracy Paul Pitts featured in his solo show *We've Never Met, But I Think About You All the Time* at the Erickson Gallery, Portland, Oregon, February 2017.

"It Takes Time, They Tell Me" is for Carol Christensen, with deep gratitude.

ACKNOWLEDGMENTS

Gratitude to the editors of the following literary journals for giving these poems (at times in earlier versions or with variant titles) their first audience:

Clackamas Literary Review: "For Lack of What Is Found There," "Grammar Lesson," "Premonition"

Cloudbank: "Against Reading," "Bed," "Blossom," "Green Couch"

Five Points: "*Funeral in Vermont*"

The Georgia Review: "Against Summer," "As If Written by the Other Woman"

Gramma: "At the Gym," "Dust," "Evening Meal"

Hubbub: "Afterwards I see everything"

I-70 Review: "A Year after the Divorce, I Take a Long Drive," "Against Detritus," "Garden Wedding"

Kosmos Quarterly: "Glide"

New Ohio Review: "And Later I Will Forget about the Bread," "Against Silence," "At the Outpatient Clinic"

The Pedestal Magazine: "A Story I Did Not Tell"

Poetry Northwest: "Two"

RHINO: "'Mind Is East Hidden by Trees'"

Snake Nation Review: "Drive-In"

Solstice: "Music"

Sou'wester: "636 Lyons Avenue, Apartment 1A," "A Story about the Heart," "A Thing or Two," "Against the Law," "Stepping into the Bathtub"

Spillway: "Before I Knew the Diagnosis," "Dead End," "First Snow," "It Takes Time, They Tell Me," "The Rules"

The Timberline Review: "Doubt," "Envy," "Nomenclature"

VoiceCatcher: "The Laws of Physics"

Vox Populi: "Arkansas to Oregon," "Betrayals," "Pleasure," "Room to Room," "The Before and the After"

Water-Stone Review: "*Contrition*"

Windfall: "Why I Kept Walking," "Living Alone at Sixty-Four"

"*Funeral in Vermont*" was featured on *Verse Daily* on February 9, 2016.

"First Snow" also appears in *The Pushcart Prize Anthology XL: Best of the Small Presses*, Bill Henderson, ed. Pushcart Press, 2016

"Against Detritus," "Against Reading," "Against Silence," and "At the Outpatient Clinic" were performed by Brooke Budy at Poetry Press Week, Portland, Oregon, June 20, 2015.

APPRECIATIONS

Observant readers will note that the poem "Room to Room" specifically describes a lost painting whose image nevertheless graces the cover of *Blue Mistaken for Sky*. After the poem was written and the manuscript completed, the painting, *Anniversary*, was located, thanks to Nisi Sturgis and Rebekah Scallet. Both Brooke Budy, the artist, and I are grateful.

Most of these poems were written in Portland, Oregon, where I moved in 2011 after living in the Arkansas Ozarks for many years. I am fortunate to have been welcomed by the vibrant and generous literary community in this city. Shout-outs to Sandra Williams of Mountain Writers Series and David Biespiel of The Attic Institute of Arts and Letters, both of whom invited me to teach workshops at their prestigious literary centers and featured me at public readings.

My sincere thanks to Literary Arts, which awarded me the 2013 Poetry Fellowship that provided time to write, and to the Multnomah County Library's Sterling Room for Writers, where initial drafts of many of these poems were composed.

I spent the spring semester of 2014 as the Visiting Poet-in-Residence at Westminster College in Salt Lake City, Utah. Gratitude to the faculty and students there for the hospitality they extended, and to local poets Lisa Bickmore, Paisley Rekdal, Natasha Sajé, Susan Sample, and Jennifer Tonge, who invited me to join their monthly critique sessions while I was in residence.

For their helpful comments on some of these poems, I thank Margaret Chula, KC Conway, Christine Delea, Cindy Williams Gutiérrez, Diane Holland, Donna Prinzmetal, Justin Rigamonti, Joanna Rose, Penelope Scambly Schott, and Suzanne Sigafoos.

Because they read and responded to the entire manuscript in great detail, I am beholden to John Brehm, Brooke Budy, and Paulann Petersen—and to Chana Bloch, who died in 2017 and who is greatly missed.

For their superlative support and wise counsel, I am indebted to Executive Editor Christine Stroud and her staff at Autumn House Press, as well as to Founding Editor Michael Simms. I am privileged to be among their authors.

ABOUT THE AUTHOR

Andrea Hollander is the author of four previous full-length poetry collections and three chapbooks. Her many honors include two Pushcart Prizes (in poetry and literary nonfiction), two poetry fellowships from the National Endowment for the Arts, the Nicholas Roerich Poetry Prize, the D. H. Lawrence Fellowship, the *Runes* Poetry Award, the *Ellipsis* Prize, the Vern Rutsala Award, an individual artist fellowship from Literary Arts of Oregon, and two fellowships in poetry from the Arkansas Arts Council. Since her retirement after twenty-two years as the Writer-in-Residence at Lyon College in Arkansas, she has lived in Portland, Oregon, where she conducts creative writing tutorials, seminars, and workshops. Her website is www.andreahollander.net.